TRAINS

TRA

A PHOTOGRAPHIC TOUR

INS
OF AMERICA'S RAILWAYS

Text and photographs by
BRIAN SOLOMON

GRAMERCY BOOKS
NEW YORK

Published by Gramercy Books, an imprint of Random House Value Publishing, a division of Random House, Inc., New York.

Gramercy is a registered trademark and the colophon is a trademark of Random House, Inc.

Random House
New York • Toronto • London • Sydney • Auckland
www.randomhouse.com

Editor: Celeste Sollod
Art director: Christine Kell
Interior designer: Carol Malcolm Russo/Signet M Design, Inc.

Printed and bound in Singapore

Library of Congress Cataloging-in-Publication Data

Solomon, Brian, 1966-
    Trains / Brian Solomon.
        p. cm.
    ISBN 0-517-22260-4
    1. Railroads—United States—Trains—Pictorial works. 2. Photgraphy of railroads—United States.
  I. Title.

TF550.S68 2004
385'.0973'022—dc22

                                                                        2003057107

10 9 8 7 6 5 4 3 2 1

All photographs by Brian Solomon unless otherwise credited:

Page 4: Photo by Robert A. Buck
Page 5: Photo by Otto Perry, Denver Public Library Western History Department. OP-19408.
Page 10-11: photo by George C. Corey
Page 14: bottom photo, Jay Williams Collection
Page 17: Brochure at bottom from the collection of Richard Jay Solomon.
Page 23: Both illustrations from the collection of Richard Jay Solomon.
Page 26: Photo by Richard Jay Solomon.
Page 28: Photo by Richard Jay Solomon.
Page 29: Photo by Richard Jay Solomon.

In Memory of Helen Burton

Acknowledgments

Photographing trains is a passion I inherited from and share with my father, Richard J. Solomon. He taught me from an early age both to appreciate the thrill of a passing train and the techniques needed to capture the experience on film. I have been trackside with camera in hand since age 5, which means that I have more than 30 years experience behind me.

In addition to my own photographs, a number of my father's images appear in this book, as well as those from Robert A. Buck, George C. Corey, and historical photos from the collections of the Denver Public Library and Jay Williams.

In my never-ending quest for railway photos, I have traveled with many fellow photographers, railway enthusiasts and others, all of whom have lent their expertise, suggested locations, and provided invaluable information necessary in the making of the photographs portrayed here. I owe many thanks and gratitude to: John Gruber, Mel Patrick, T.S. Hoover, Tom M. Hoover, Dick Gruber, Brian Jennison, George S. Pitarys, Don Marson, Mike Gardner, Tim Doherty, Patrick Yough, Dave Burton, Mike Danneman, Tom Danneman, Carl Swanson, Doug Riddell, John P. Hankey, Paul Hammond, J.D. Schmid, Ed Beaudette, Steve Carlson, Mike Abalos, Charlie Streetman, Erik Hendrickson, Howard Ande, F.L. Becht, Gerald Hook, Mike Blaszak, Brian Rutherford, Clark Johnson, Claire Nolan, Mike Confalone, Hal Miller, Doug Moore, and Brandon Delany. Special thanks to Mike Gardner for allowing me to use his darkroom and studio facilities, to Doug Moore for assistance with copywork, to the Irish Railway Record Society for use of their library, also to my brother, Seán Solomon, and my mother Maureen. Thanks to my editor Celeste Sollod who suggested the topic for this book and to the artists and production people who made it possible.

Introduction: America's Trains

The majesty of trains is part of the mystique of the railway. Since trains were developed in the 1820s, they have captured the public imagination. These mechanical beasts of burden move across the landscape, day and night, carrying people, freight, and mail. The sight of a train—be it an antique preserved steam locomotive, a mile-long iron ore drag, or the most modern high-speed passenger train—stirs all of us, reminding us of places we've been and places we'll go.

The Railway Shapes America

The earliest railways were primitive industrial tramways in Britain used for moving coal, stone, and iron ore. A few such railways were built in America during the early part of the nineteenth century. These lines originally used animals to haul short trains of loosely coupled wagons.

One product of the industrial revolution that began in the 1700s was the steam engine. In the early 1800s, experimental steam locomotives were built in England for use on the industrial railways. Within twenty years, the steam-powered tramway had been expanded into the steam-powered public railway. During the late 1820s, American engineers traveled to England to learn about the science of railways, and they brought back the basic components of railway technology: iron rails and steam locomotives.

In 1830, New York businessman Peter Cooper organized the construction of a small one-ton demonstration locomotive to convince the newly formed Baltimore & Ohio Rail Road that practical locomotives could be designed and manufactured in the United States. Unlike British railways, which were built to very high standards with relatively straight and level rights of way that were fenced off and patrolled, American lines used lightly built track, with sharp curves, that was largely unfenced. Animals would wander onto the tracks, posing a hazard to trains (not to mention the animals themselves). To accommodate the rougher, more sinuous track structure, American locomotives were fitted with pilot wheels to improve tracking ability on curves and

Opposite: After pausing for water at Cresco, Cumbres & Toltec 463 resumes its ascent of Cumbres Pass, a 10,000-foot high crossing of the Rockies near the New Mexico-Colorado state line. C&T 463 is a narrow-gauge Mikado-type steam locomotive built in 1903 by Baldwin for Rio Grande's three-foot gauge lines. It is known colloquially as a "Mud Hen" because of its reputation for stirring up the ballast as it worked Colorado's mountain grades. Today, Cumbres & Toltec operates a 64-mile section of the old Rio Grande narrow gauge as a preserved railway.

Above: *"Tom Thumb," designed by engineer and philanthropist Peter Cooper (who also invented Jell-O®), was a small demonstration locomotive built in 1830 to convince the Baltimore & Ohio that steam locomotives could be built domestically. The original machine weighed just one ton, so years after it was scrapped, shrouded in myth, it became known as the "Tom Thumb" after the popular diminutive circus entertainer.*

Below: *In the Victorian period locomotives were colorful and elaborately decorated machines. A detailed side view of the headlamp of locomotive William Crooks shows the ornate decoration used at this time. In later years locomotives took on a more spartan character.*

minimize the chance of derailment. They also incorporated fixed pilots—often described as "cow catchers"—plow-like devices to keep animals and debris from getting under the wheels of the train. Later locomotives were fitted with warning devices, such as bells, whistles, and headlamps.

Until the 1870s and 1880s, wood was the most common fuel for locomotives. In the Victorian age, railways decorated their locomotives and cars ornately, often using complex patterns and bright colors to adorn the machinery. The switch to coal in the late nineteenth century, in combination with changing attitudes toward business and labor practices, largely put an end to the ornate decor and coloring of locomotives. By the 1890s, American locomotives were normally dressed in utilitarian black paint, a feature that characterized steam locomotives until they were phased out in the 1940s and 1950s. Passenger cars, especially those used on the deluxe limiteds, often featured elaborate decor, voluptuous furnishings, and the rich styles of the Victorian and Edwardian periods.

Passenger Trains

To the accountants, poring over the ledgers of company affairs, passenger traffic was always the lesser part of railroad business, but to the public, passenger trains defined the railroad. Passenger trains revolutionized travel by dramatically reducing the time it took to get somewhere. The thrill of riding trains has long been one of the great pleasures of modern travel. Railway travel opens new horizons, provides the opportunity to meet people, and allows the passenger to experience motion without being consumed by it.

The earliest railway passenger cars were little more than horse carriages adapted for railway service. Basic coaches evolved, and as the length of trains increased and railway traveled matured, specialized passenger equipment developed. By the 1860s, there was a demand for sleeping cars, and a whole business developed around the construction, maintenance and operation of railway sleeping cars. The best known sleeping car companies were

Opposite: The steam locomotive, once a symbol of progress, now evokes nostalgia for a bygone time. An East Broad Top Mikado, a typical early twentieth-century locomotive, steams in the morning sun at Rockhill Furnace, Pennsylvania.

Boston & Albany's Lima-built Berkshire 1448 engine leads an eastbound freight train in Warren, Massachusetts. The Berkshire was the first type of steam Superpower engine, which characterized one of the last phases of steam locomotive development.

Wagner and Pullman. As late as the 1950s, thousands of Pullman cars provided night services between most cities in North America. Sadly, Pullman services declined along with the passenger services during the following decade. Today, a few sleeping cars are still operated in the United States, but they, like passenger trains, are now owned and operated by Amtrak.

Another type of specialized passenger car is the diner, which became a standard feature on long-distance passenger trains after about 1890. A diner featured a complete rolling kitchen complete with highly trained staff. Meals in the diner were not the cheapest, but were often of very high quality. They were served on specially issued china and with cutlery that featured patterns and markings specifically for the railway that was providing the service. Diners were not just a convenience for passengers, but offered railroads a way of making some extra money. Diners also helped define a railroad's passenger service. Railroads that had an inferior route

between major cities, perhaps because of geographical impediments, could compete for passenger traffic by providing superior dining car service. After all, what's an extra hour or two travel time if you are enjoying the ride?

Railroads sold the concept of quality to their passengers and advertised their best trains on the quality of journey. Many railroads offered a variety of trains between common points that provided various levels of service. On the high-end of long-distance travel were deluxe "extra-fare" limiteds—the very best name trains; in the middle were secondary trains, those that operated on express schedules but did not carry the status of the better known trains; and near the bottom were all-stops trains and the "milk-runs" that served every little hamlet along the way (and actually carried milk).

Around major cities, railroads found that they could make good money by moving the same people twice a day to and from work. Commuter trains helped to create the first suburban communities. Boston was the first city

Union Pacific's City of Denver *is seen at Denver Union Station. UP ordered a fleet of diesel-electric high-speed streamlined trains in the 1930s in an effort to win passengers back to its long-distance routes.*

to enjoy a large suburban commuter service. Commuter trains met a different need than long-distance trains, and they took on different characteristics. Today modern commuter trains are more spartan and functional than long-distance trains. The commuter does not demand the comfort or catering of a long-distance passenger.

Related to commuter railways were various types of electric railways and urban transit systems. The first urban rail-transit was horse-drawn streetcar lines. In the 1870s and 1880s, some cities developed cable-car routes. Of these, Chicago had the most extensive network, but they could also be found in New York, Seattle, and of course, San Francisco, the first and most famous city to use them. Elevated, steam-powered, rapid transit lines were built in New York and Chicago. After 1900, rapid transit elevated lines were electrified and later integrated with subterranean metropolitan railways—subways. The New York City subway is the best known of these rapid transit systems and was created from an amalgam of various private and public operators.

In the 1880s, the electrically powered trolley car first made its appearance. By the 1890s, hundreds of light electric railways had been built and were running electric streetcars down the main streets of cities in every state. In the early years of the twentieth century, the lightly built street railway concept was expanded into interurban electric railways that connected cities and small towns, often running on roadsides, and competing directly with the larger, established steam railroads. Electric operations allowed for the development of a new kind of iron horse; the electric locomotive.

Freight Trains

Since their beginning, railways have been involved in the movement of freight. Passenger trains captured much of the glory, but freight trains usually earned big profits. Many railway lines have been built solely with designs on freight traffic.

In the first decades of American railroading, freight and passenger trains both operated at relatively slow speeds by contemporary standards. Rough track, brittle rails, small locomotives, and primitive scheduling as the only practical means for train separation usually meant that trains plodded along at just 20 to 30 miles per hour. As railway technology advanced, speeds increased. By the 1890s, railways had broken the 100 mph mark in test runs. Railways were regularly operating fast passenger trains at top speeds of 70 and 80 mph. By contrast, as late as 1920, the average speed of a freight train had not improved significantly since the 1840s, with some low priority trains only averaging 8 miles per hour over the road. Moving freight in long slow chains of cars required larger more powerful locomotives than used for passenger trains.

Wide open spaces, thriving industry, larger clearances, and profit-driven railroad companies gradually pushed the size of freight trains to extremes. As early as the 1840s, the Western Railroad of Massachusetts was running trains with as many as sixty freight cars. The remarkable thing is that this was before the advent of automatic airbrakes; brakes were set manually by strong brakemen, who literally rode the tops of the cars waiting for a "down brakes" signal from the engineer. To set the brakes, they would quickly turn down large iron wheels located on each car, jumping from one car to the next as the train rolled along. This was dangerous work in good weather and truly hazardous in bad. This primitive system was one of the reasons that freight train speeds remained so slow for so long. The eventual universal adoption of airbrake-equipped freight cars, along with other safety improvements such as the automatic coupler and automatic block signalling, allowed railroads to increase both the size and speed of freight runs.

Bigger, faster freight trains required more powerful locomotives. From the mid-1890s until the mid-1940s, American railroads pushed the steam locomotive to its ultimate size. Where Peter Cooper's experimental locomotive had weighed just one ton, and the typical American-type steam engine from the 1850s may have weighed 30 tons, the largest steam locomotives of the 1940s, Union Pacific's famed Big Boy and Chesapeake & Ohio's massive Allegheny, weighed 386 tons and 387.7 tons respectively. More common locomotives weighed less than these monsters, but were still big in comparison with the early machines.

Larger locomotives were needed for a variety of reasons. Originally most railway cars were made primarily of wood. In the early days this was the logical material to build cars from because it was easy to work with and the builders of horse-drawn carriages were familiar with it. The problem with wooden railway cars is that they disintegrate in the event of a collision. This issue was most severe in regards to passenger cars. First, steel frame cars were required, and by the World War I period, it was a Federal regulation that all new passenger cars use steel frames and steel bodies. Eventually freight cars were also built with steel frames, and then all-steel construction.

Steel freight cars increased the weight of trains, requiring more power to haul them. Also, steel-framed freight cars allowed railroads to run much longer trains than had been practical with all-wood cars. The size of cars grew too. In the 1920s, the 30-foot boxcar was standard. By the 1940s, boxcars had grown to 40 feet, then they grew to 50 feet. In some cases boxcars are now built up to 80 feet long. More powerful locomotives were also needed when railroads finally decided to increase freight train speed.

The need for a powerful locomotive that could run relatively fast with a heavy train encouraged locomotive builders to push the limits of steam technology. In the mid-1920s, a new and innovative locomotive builder, Lima, introduced a more powerful new type of locomotive which it called "Superpower." A superpowered steam locomotive had a much greater firebox and boiler capacity than earlier types and thus could haul a heavy load at faster speeds without lost of power due to low steam pressure.

Railroad Evolution

From the 1930s onward, American railroads underwent a striking metamorphosis in the face of great competition. In just a few decades the passenger train had gone from being the foremost method of travel to one of the more obscure. In the 1920s, American railroads noticed the effects of growing highway competition, and by the mid-1930s the effects of the private automobile, bus, and airplane, combined with the disastrous implications of the Great Depression, caused passenger ridership to drop sharply. To counter these losses, some railroads developed new high-speed streamlined passenger trains to make railway travel more exciting—and more profitable. Union Pacific and Burlington debuted America's first streamliners in 1934. These lightweight diesel-powered machines were the antithesis of the traditional steam-powered heavyweight passenger train. Streamlined trains combined the latest construction techniques with flashy Art Deco designs. By the late 1930s, streamlined trains were a great success and many railroads used them to spiff up their long-distance services. They also spawned great interest in the prowess of diesel-electric locomotives.

From 1941 to 1945, during World War II, American railroads hustled to move the greatest amount of traffic they had ever carried. During this time many railroads were compelled by the government to order steam locomotives because the materials needed for diesel locomotives were allocated for war munitions. Following World War II, American railroads fell on difficult times again. Widespread private car ownership and the construction of the Interstate Highway System starting in the late 1950s hit railroads hard. In the postwar years, railroads abandoned the steam locomotive in an effort to cut costs and ordered ever more powerful diesels. The last regular mainline steam operations ended in 1960, although some locomotives were preserved for excursions, display, and museum operation.

The end of steam was followed by the last runs of many famous passenger trains, as railroads curtailed services in the wake of declining demand and growing passenger train deficits. In 1971, the Federal Government created Amtrak to relieve freight railroads of their obligations to provide long-distance passenger services. With the coming of Amtrak, the number of routes was scaled back drastically. Over the next decade, most commuter runs were taken over by state agencies and transit authorities.

Railroads Today

Passenger trains have evolved in the last thirty years. Amtrak uses primarily high-level Superliner equipment for its western long-distance runs, while assigning various type of modern low-level equipment to its eastern runs and shorter hauls. In 2000, Amtrak introduced its fastest service, the *Acela Express*, which uses state-of-the-art double-ended streamlined electric trains to connect Boston, New York, and Washington D.C. These trains are capable of up to 150 mph in regular service on designated sections of the route.

Meanwhile, freight railroads underwent a different sort of transformation. From the 1960s onward, a succession of corporate mergers consumed traditional companies, resulting in just a few large mega-systems. The traditional names gave way to corporate amalgamations; for example, the old Baltimore & Ohio is now a component of CSX, and the Santa Fe is a part of Burlington Northern Santa Fe. As the companies combined, the number of lines was trimmed. The new large companies looked to achieve savings by eliminating redundant lines and selling or abandoning unprofitable secondary lines and branches.

Southern Pacific's suburban passenger trains between San Francisco and San Jose were always known as "Commutes." Today this popular service is now operated by CalTrain, a public agency. Against the back drop of the San Francisco skyline, a Commute departs Fourth and Townsend for San Jose.

Above: The Rio Grande railway was built as a narrow gauge line which connected mining communities in Colorado, Utah, and New Mexico in the 1870s and 1880s. While many of its lines were later converted to standard gauge operations, some steam-powered narrow gauge routes remained in commercial use until the late 1960s. Today tourist lines, such as the Cumbres & Toltec seen here at Chama, New Mexico, operate portions of the old Rio Grande narrow gauge.

Opposite: Saginaw Timber No. 2 is lightweight Mikado-type locomotive built for moving timber. The Mikado was one of the most common steam locomotive types built in the early twentieth century. This one is preserved at North Freedom, Wisconsin.

The spin-off of secondary routes and branch lines led to the formation of many new railroads, most of which are short lines. A short line is a railroad that operates less than 300 miles of track and generates a relatively small amount of traffic. In addition to short lines, some spin-offs resulted in larger "regional railroads" that operate more than 300 miles of track, yet are still relatively small in comparison with the mega-systems. By the late 1990s, there were hundreds of small freight railroads operating branch lines all over the country.

Despite the large number of short lines, most inter-city freight traffic is now handled by just six large railroads: CSX, Norfolk Southern, Union Pacific, Burlington Northern Santa Fe, Canadian Pacific, and Canadian National, the last two lines each having bought up several traditional American railroads. These mega-railroads haul a tremendous volume of bulk freight. In the 1980s, new types of freight cars were developed that allow containers to be stacked two high. Whole trains of containers are moved using these double-stack cars, and consist of as many as 200 units, so can carry up to 400 containers. New types of diesel engines were developed that are much more powerful than those of the 1940s and 1950s. Modern diesels have a utilitarian, no-frills appearance. These machines are money-makers and judged by their power and reliability rather than their style.

Railroads are still a crucial part of America's life, her industry, and her history. Trains still offer the thrill of adventure and travel, of moving across wide-open spaces and into the heart of big cities. Although railroads have lost their transportation supremacy, their unique romance remains.

Until the mid-1950s, Boston & Maine used venerable Moguls, one of the last steam locomotives in regular service in New England, to haul suburban passenger services on its Central Mass route west of Boston. At the time of this photo, near the end of its service life, the locomotive had been working for four decades.

Above: Between the 1890s and World War I, lightweight interurban electric railways connecting small towns and cities were built all over the United States. While most of these lines were abandoned from the 1920s onward, a few, such as this line used for freight switching in Mason City, Iowa, have survived as traditional electric operations.

Above: In the early days of train travel in the nineteenth century, passenger cars were generally made of wood. Later designs, such as those pictured here at North Freedom, Wisconsin, incorporated steel frames for improved structural strength in case of accidents. By the 1910s, all-steel equipment was becoming standard for intercity journeys, yet wood-bodied cars survived on branch lines.

Opposite: Chicago & North Western No. 1385 is typical of the ten-wheeler types used for freight and passenger services in the early years of the twentieth century. Bumped from mainline work by the 1930s by heavier, more powerful steam locomotives, ten-wheelers often worked rural branch lines until the mid-1950s.

Top: The Consolidation type locomotive was among the most numerous steam locomotives built for freight service. The type was first built in the 1860s and had become popular by 1900. Western Maryland Scenic Railway operates a vintage Consolidation in excursion service between Cumberland and Frostburg, Maryland.

◆

Bottom: Baltimore & Ohio Mikado locomotives doublehead a freight at Grafton, West Virginia. Doubleheading—working two steam locomotives on one train— was common practice on many lines in the steam era, especially where steep grades required lots of power to keep trains moving. Each steam locomotive required its own crew, an expensive practice. Today two or more diesels are routinely operated together under the control of a common throttle, thus allowing one crew to do more work.

◆

Opposite: Duluth & Northern, Minnesota No. 14 is Baldwin-built Mikado, typical of locomotives built in the first decades of twentieth century. The Mikado was a standard workhorse locomotive, and thousands of its type were used in freight services all across the United States until displaced by diesels in the 1940s and 1950s.

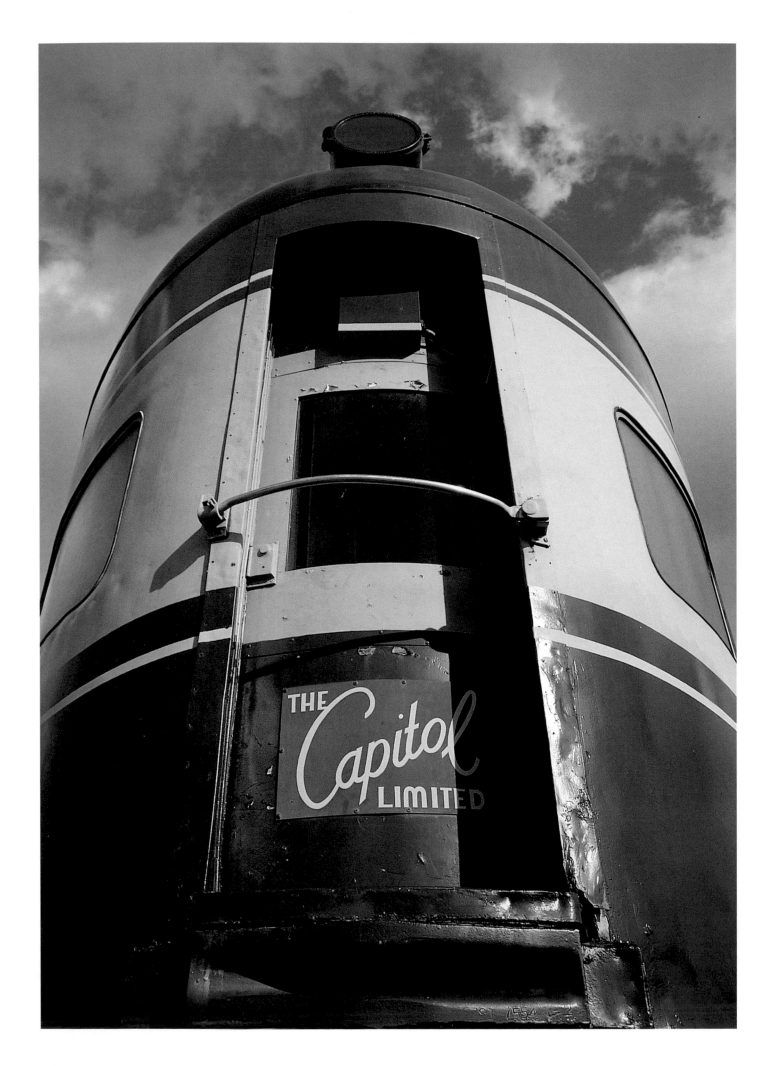

Above: One of the finest ways to travel is by private railroad car. Hundreds of these deluxe cars, such as the *Caritas* run by High Iron Travel, still operate on American rails. Originally a sleeping car for the St. Louis & San Francisco "The Frisco Lines," *Caritas* was rebuilt in the Art Deco style in the 1980s.

Left: This Pennsylvania Railroad brochure from 1934 celebrates 100 years of progress in American railroading. The train on top represents one used by an early Pennsylvania Railroad predecessor, while the locomotive at the bottom is a PRR K4s Pacific-type, one of the best known American steam locomotives.

Opposite: Round-end observation cars were the modern streamlined successor to the traditional open-end observation cars popular in the later steam era. Baltimore & Ohio's *Capitol Limited* offered an overnight service between Washington D.C. and Chicago by way of Pittsburgh. This style of car was built from the late 1930s until the early 1950s.

Pages 18-19: In the 1930s, Southern Pacific introduced its famous *Daylight* streamlined passenger trains. Leading this historic *Daylight* train through Ericson, California, is SP streamlined Lima-Northern No. 4449, considered to be one of finest locomotives ever built.

Milwaukee Road, short for the Chicago, Milwaukee, St. Paul & Pacific railroad, was a midwestern granger line—a railroad that served the breadbasket of America—that eventually went all the way to the Pacific coast. The Northern type locomotive was a classic example of "Superpower" steam, which had great boiler capacity to maintain great power at speed. In 1944, Milwaukee Road bought ten Class S-3 Northerns from Alco, including No. 261. Today it is still in service as a popular excursion locomotive based in the Twin Cities.

Above: In 1941, Alco developed the model RS-1, the first "road-switcher" type diesel electric locomotive. The road-switcher later became the most common and most versatile style of locomotive. The RS-1 was designed for general use and was equally suited for yard work sorting cars, branch line freight and passenger service, or main-line work. Fifty years after the type was introduced, Green Mountain Alco RS-1 405 was photographed at Chester, Vermont, in October 1991.

Above, right: With the decline of steam power, steam builder Baldwin Locomotive Works tried its talents constructing diesels during the 1940s and 1950s. Unfortunately, its success as a steam builder did not transfer over to diesel and the company exited the locomotive-building business in the 1950s. Their most successful diesels were switchers.

Opposite: Union Pacific's last steam locomotive was Alco-built Northern No. 844, first made during World War II. This locomotive was never retired. It is still used for passenger excursions and occasionally for freight work, as seen here in Cheyenne, Wyoming, in 1989.

Page 24: General Motors' Electro-Motive Division was the most successful diesel locomotive manufacturer in the twentieth century. Electro-Motive's "Bull Dog nose" typified diesel-electric locomotives built in the 1940s and 1950s. Illinois Central No. 100 is a model F9 reserved for the line's deluxe executive passenger train.

Top: Electro-Motive E-units were fast streamlined diesels used to haul passenger trains such as this attractively painted Pere Marquette streamliner seen in a period postcard view from the late 1940s. Streamliners were introduced in the 1930s to attract passengers. Pere Marquette was a Michigan-based railway later absorbed by the Chesapeake & Ohio.

Bottom: This period postcard depicts Southern Pacific and Rock Island's *Golden State*—a typical 1950s-era streamlined passenger train—that connected Chicago and Los Angeles by way of Tucumcari, New Mexico. After World War II, many lines added new streamliners and the *Golden State* was one of the many popular ones. Both period postcards on this page exemplify a style popular in the 1940s and 1950s.

Above: Both trains in these photographs use equipment built during the streamlined era; the Conway Scenic excursion trains are still in service today. The author's mother enjoys the view from a Vista Dome operating on the *North Coast Limited*, a streamlined long-distance passenger train traveling across the plains of eastern Montana.

Right: The Conway Scenic operates excursion trains with former Canadian National Railways streamlined F-unit diesels over the old Maine Central Mountain Division through New Hampshire's Crawford Notch in the White Mountains.

In the 1960s, the Reading Company resurrected five of its big T-1 Northern-type steam locomotives for excursion work. A "Reading Ramble" is seen on a damp day in eastern Pennsylvania in October 1964. Reading is probably best known for its place on the Monopoly game board.

Above: Norfolk & Western was the last American railroad to build and operate steam locomotives in heavy service. In 1957, an N&W Mallet compound hauls a heavily laden coal train over Virginia's Blue Ridge Summit. The Mallet used two sets of cylinders under a common boiler. In the early years of the twentieth century this was considered a technological advance in heavy locomotive design. N&W was the last American railroad to build and use Mallets; it maintained them in regular service until 1960.

❧

Pages 30-31: Keeping tracks clear requires special equipment. In March 1991, Southern Pacific clears Donner Pass high in the California Sierra with a snow-service Jordan spreader pushed by a pair of Electro-Motive GP38s. Named for the ill-fated Donner party who were trapped on the east slope, this Sierra pass was later the route of the first transcontinental railroad, completed in 1869. Donner is legendary for its exceptionally heavy snowfall, which has exceeded 700 inches a year.

At one time Donner Pass, shown on pages 30-31, was the premier railway routing to California, but now it has taken a back seat to lines in southern California, such as SP's Sunset Route. Here, three high output Electro-Motive GP60s lead a double-stack container train at Redlands, California. This train is seen against the backdrop of the San Gabriel mountains. Double stacking containers was promoted in the 1980s and effectively doubled the capacity of a freight train, giving railroads an advantage in moving transcontinental traffic.

Opposite: Changes in railroad rate-regulation in the 1980s shifted freight traffic routes. While lines such as Southern Pacific's Sunset Route (pictured on page 32) blossomed with new business, other routes such as the Canadian Pacific line across the top of Maine withered. In the 1990s, Canadian Pacific sold its line across the state of Maine to short line operators including the Canadian American. In October 1997, an eastbound Canadian American freight nears the old railroad location known as Camp 12, east of Greenville, Maine. In the 1960s a dozen daily trains used the CP route, but today there is just one short train in each direction.

◆

Above: The Vermont Rail System operates portions of the old Rutland Railroad. In February 2002, a freshly painted Electro-Motive GP60 leads the daily Vermont Rail System freight from Rutland to Bellows Falls, Vermont, near Mt. Holly. Twenty years ago this line hosted short freights hauled by old Green Mountain RS-1s (see page 22). By 2002, business had boomed. Daily trains often had more than 90 cars, which required locomotives such as GP60s, three times more powerful than the RS-1s, for the climb over Mt. Holly Summit.

◆

Pages 36-37: Vermont Railway is a component of the Vermont Rail System. The company uses a variety of second-hand Electro-Motive road switchers to haul its freight trains. Here Vermont Railway Electro-Motive diesels are seen near Chester, Vermont. Vermont Railway's herald symbolically represents the state's Green Mountain range. In winter heavy snow can make operations in the mountains more challenging. Sometimes railroad plows are called out to clear the tracks ahead of the freight trains. (See also pages 30-31.)

Opposite: Short lines are relatively small railways that typically operate branch lines or are contracted for switching operations, in which freight cars are sorted and placed on sidings for customers. Chicago Short Line is an appropriately named company that works industrial lines in the southeastern part of the Windy City. This Electro-Motive switcher features a low-profile cab, giving it better clearance in industrial areas.

Left and below: Louisiana & Delta is a short line that began operation in 1986 on former Southern Pacific branch lines in central Louisiana using former Santa Fe CF7 diesels. In the 1970s Santa Fe rebuilt many of its old Electro-Motive F-units, making them into more versatile road-switchers, which it designated CF7s. In the 1980s, Santa Fe sold many CF7s to newly formed short line railways. Louisiana & Delta is one of several short lines in the Genessee & Wyoming family of railways.

The legendary locomotive engineer Casey Jones ran trains for Illinois Central before his untimely demise in 1900 behind the throttle of engine 638—an event that inspired the "Ballad of Casey Jones." On a sunny morning some 96 years later, an Illinois Central freight rolls northward at Zachary, Louisiana. In the 1990s, a series of company mergers gobbled up many traditional railroads. Today, the old IC is part of Canadian National Railway.

Electro-Motive diesels lead a westbound Kansas City Southern intermodal freight just west of the Mississippi River crossing at Vickburg, Mississippi. Intermodal trains carry piggyback truck trailers and containers that can be hauled by train, truck, ship or plane—thus the term "intermodal."

When locomotives reach the end of their service lives, they are salvaged of usable parts and cut up for scrap. The cab of an Electro-Motive road switcher is seen in Wisconsin Central's scrap line at Fond du Lac, Wisconsin. Often locomotives serve for 20 years or more before they are scrapped.

Opposite, top: The geography and post-industrial economy of New England has made it a difficult place to make money in railroading. New England Central took over operations of the former Central Vermont Railway in 1995. This line connects St. Albans, Vermont, with New London, Connecticut, operating freight service and accommodating Amtrak's daily *Vermonter*. New England Central freight No. 608 is seen at the summit of State Line Hill, in Monson, Massachusetts. This train runs daily between Palmer, Massachusetts, and New London using Electro-Motive GP38s.

Opposite, bottom: Trains run in all weather. General Electric C30-7As lead a westbound Conrail freight up the east slope of the Berkshires on the former Boston & Albany mainline where Lima's Berkshire-type steam locomotives once worked (see page 4). Rain makes rails slippery and this heavy freight lost traction and stalled. Locomotives from another train were needed to get it moving again.

Above: A Central Vermont Railway local freight works the interchange track at Palmer, Massachusetts, in 1987. This train of 50-foot boxcars is led by CV's 1950s vintage Electro-Motive GP9 diesels. The GP9 was one of the most popular of Electro-Motive's "General Purpose" line introduced in 1949 after the success of Alco's RS1 and similar types.

Pages 46-47: A Union Pacific grain train rolls west near North Platte, Nebraska. Leading is an Electro-Motive SD60M featuring a North American Safety Cab. This cab was introduced in 1989 to provide a place for crew members to sit after the elimination of the caboose, the rolling office that traditionally marked the tail end of freight trains. Today the "wide nose" Safety Cab is standard on most new locomotives. Union Pacific's main line across Nebraska is a primary conduit for transcontinental freight traffic, often handling more than 80 trains a day.

A Kansas City Southern freight climbs over the Mississippi River at Baton Rouge, Louisiana. While KCS operates some intermodal trains (see page 42), much of its business is carried in more traditional freight cars, such as the 50-foot long box cars pictured on this train.

Looking west across the Mississippi at Vicksburg at sunset, we find an eastbound Kansas City Southern freight rolling across a bridge once owned by Illinois Central, and later short line Midsouth, before KCS took over the route. In the last decade this east-west route has developed into an important gateway for freight trains. Today, Kansas City Southern is one of the last traditional names in modern railroading. Most once familiar names have disappeared as a result of merger and consolidation. The Pennsylvania Railroad, Santa Fe, Southern Pacific, Boston & Maine, and Northern Pacific are all gone.

A pair of Burlington Northern's Electro-Motive model SD60M "Safety Cabs" lead a very heavy train of hot taconite pellets near Hibbing, Minnesota. Iron ore from the Minnesota Iron Range is moved by rail to Lake Superior ports where it is transferred to boats for shipment across the Great Lakes.

Southern Pacific's "Oil Cans" was a daily movement of crude oil from Bakersfield to Long Beach, California. This train was effectively a rolling pipeline consisting of dozens of tank cars linked together with pipes to facilitate rapid loading and unloading. It is seen at Monolith, near Tehachapi Summit.

Above: Lumber cars roll through California's Salinas Valley on Southern Pacific's Coast Line. Timber products are one of the many commodities hauled by American freight railroads, and often moved on specialized freight cars.

❖

Left: In California, Southern Pacific hauled solid trains of sugar beets from the fields where they were grown to sugar processing plants. Until the 1990s, the beets were hauled in traditional wooden-bodied cars known to railroaders as "beet racks." These cars were among the last wooden cars in regular service in the United States.

❖

Pages 54-55: The Napa Valley Wine Train began running in 1989. This classy excursion train caters to up-market diners and wine connoisseurs. It operates through California's Napa Valley using traditional passenger cars led by Montreal Locomotive Works FPA-4 diesels built in the 1950s. The locomotives and antique cars give the train a nostalgic quality that appeals to its riders. The line is a former Southern Pacific branch to St. Helena, California.

California Northern is a short line company that assumed operation of several lightly used Southern Pacific freight lines in the mid-1990s. In 1994, a California Northern GP15-1 diesel rests in front of the former Northwestern Pacific station in Petaluma, California. The GP15-1 was a moderately powered diesel model built by Electro-Motive in the 1970s and 1980s. This locomotive was acquired secondhand. It was originally built for Chicago & North Western and features a snow plow, needed for clearing midwestern tracks, but of little use in Petaluma, California, where snow is a rare occurrence.

Above: An eastbound Southern Pacific freight ascends Donner Pass, high in the California Sierra mountain range, at a location east of Alta, California, known on old timetables as "Gorge." Here the rails ride on a ledge 2,000 feet above the American River Canyon. The diesels on this train were specially designed by Electro-Motive for the many tunnels and snowsheds on Donner Pass and are known colloquially as "Tunnel Motors."

Above: A westbound Southern Pacific freight climbs through tunnels and snowsheds at Donner Pass. Southern Pacific used to operate two lines over the summit. This is the original 1860s crossing, which was abandoned in 1993. Today all trains over Donner use the more modern 1920s track alignment which traverses a two-mile long tunnel under Mt. Judah to reach Donner Summit. SP was bought by Union Pacific in 1997.

Above: Union Pacific ordered hundreds of modern, microprocessor controlled "DASH 8" locomotives from General Electric in the 1980s and 1990s. A UP DASH 8 leads a freight through Nevada's remote Clover Creek Canyon. This unpopulated desert canyon characterizes the scenery of the American West. Trains have to travel across hundreds of miles of barren landscape to reach population centers of the western United States, even today.

Opposite: CalTrain 905 is an Electro-Motive built F40PH, seen at the Fourth and Townsend Street terminal, near where the famous Cirque du Soleil is making its 1991 showing in San Francisco. For many years Southern Pacific's San Francisco-San Jose commutes were the only suburban passenger trains in the West. Today, Los Angeles, San Diego, and Seattle are also served by suburban passenger trains. The bright stripes on the front of the loco-motive are a safety feature intended to make it easier to spot when approaching grade crossings.

Pages 60-61: At Thompson, Utah, Southern Pacific Electro-Motive "Tunnel Motor" diesels lead a mixed freight westward over the old Rio Grande mainline between Grand Junction and Salt Lake City, against a backdrop of the LaSalle Mountains many miles distant. Fresh snow has brightened the desert floor. This line was built as narrow gauge route from Denver in the 1880s and was later rebuilt, in part relocated, and converted to standard gauge to allow for better integration with other railroads. Today the line is a component of Union Pacific, once Rio Grande's competitor.

Petersburg, Pennsylvania, is a small community along the old Pennsylvania Railroad "Middle Division," an important freight corridor across central Pennsylvania. Today this route is operated by Norfolk Southern, who took control from Conrail in 1999. In 1997, an east-ward "Piggyback" train carries dozens of trailer truck bodies on flatcars in piggyback style. The trucks are lifted by cranes onto the flat cars for transit cross country by train. This is cheaper and more efficient than moving them over the roads.

Above: Great Northern's *Empire Builder*, its flagship train, was named for the railway's founder, the legendary James J. Hill, a man known as "The Empire Builder."

Opposite: Today, Amtrak's *Empire Builder* operates over the former Great Northern tracks between the Twin Cities of Minneapolis and St. Paul and Seattle, following the original *Empire Builder*'s route. The train is seen against the backdrop of the Rocky Mountains near Spotted Robe, Montana.

Right: In September 2000, a Batten Kill Railroad freight crosses a deck bridge at Eaglebridge, New York, near where it interchanges freight cars with Guilford's Boston & Maine line. The Batten Kill is one of many short line freight railroads operating in New York State.

Pages 68-69: East of Winnemucca, Nevada, Amtrak's modern *California Zephyr* follows much of the same route of the original train jointly run by Western Pacific, Rio Grande, and Burlington. Instead of the traditional 1950s-era Budd-built streamliner, Amtrak uses modern high-level Superliner cars, typical of equipment assigned to its western runs. West of Winnemucca, the train now uses a former Southern Pacific routing to Oakland, which sends the train over Donner Pass, rather than through the famous Feather River Canyon. In 1993, the westbound *Zephyr* is seen ascending Donner, near Truckee, California.

Right: Baltimore & Ohio was one of America's first and best-known railroads. It operated freight and passenger trains between Philadelphia, Baltimore, Washington D.C., Chicago, and St. Louis. Today, some of its Baltimore area lines host MARC commuter trains, while Amtrak provides long distance services on the old B&O Washington to Chicago route.

Opposite: A modern push-pull commuter train at Baltimore's Camden Station. Today Baltimore-area commuter trains are operated by MARC, a Maryland public transport agency. Push-pull sets feature a locomotive at one end and a control cab car at the other. In one direction the engine pushes the train, in the other it pulls. With this arrangement the locomotive engineer can safely operate the train from either end, and this greatly simplifies commuter train operations. Instead of running the engine around the train to reverse directions when it reaches a terminal station, the engineer just walks from one end to the other. Most modern commuter trains now use the push-pull arrangement.

In New York City, long-distance trains, commuter trains, and the subway provide an integrated rail transport network. A Flushing bound IRT train is seen at Queens Plaza. Interborough Rapid Transit was once a private company. Today it is a component of the New York City subway system. Traditionally subways operated underground, but later some lines were extended above ground, with many operating above city streets on elevated structures such as that pictured here. Predating the New York subways were privately operated steam-powered elevated railways. These were electrified around 1900 and eventually integrated with the New York subway system. Few of the original elevated lines remain today, and most elevated sections are subway extensions such as the Flushing Line pictured here.

Above: The Massachusetts Bay Transportation Authority operates both heavy-rail commuter trains and Boston's transit system. An MBTA commuter train running on the old Boston & Maine crosses the Merrimack River at Haverhill, Massachusetts, in March 2002.

Opposite: Metro-North operates suburban passenger services from New York's Grand Central Terminal over lines formerly run by New York Central and New Haven railroads. A Metro-North local is seen along the Hudson near Cold Spring, New York. This train is powered by an Electro-Motive FL9 locomotive built for the New Haven Railroad in the 1950s, but featuring the streamlined style developed in the 1930s.

New York, New Haven & Hartford was the first railroad to electrify its lines using high voltage overhead lines. Today this route hosts Metro-North commuter trains, such as this one photographed at Milford, Connecticut, as well as Amtrak's *Acela Regional* and *Acela Express* trains.

Traditionally New Jersey's commuter trains were run by various private railroads, including the Pennsylvania Railroad, Central Railroad of New Jersey, Lackawanna, Erie Railroad, and New York Susquehanna & Western. By the 1950s and 1960s changes in railroad economics had turned these once lucrative services in to big money losers. Suburban railways still carried tens of thousands of passengers daily, but did so at a loss. At first subsidies were provided to the private railroads, then eventually state agencies took over the operations. Today, New Jersey Transit runs suburban passenger services in that state. Other states experienced the same transition from private to public operation. Still others lost their services, to the detriment of the riders.

A Chicago Metra bi-level commuter train pauses at Highlands on the old Burlington line to Aurora, Illinois. Bi-level cars increase the capacity of commuter trains. Thousands of Chicago commuters ride such trains to work everyday, avoiding the stress of highway commuting.

Above: In the early 1960s, a New York Central long-distance train makes a station stop at Englewood on Chicago's Southside. Prior to Amtrak, Chicago was served by many different companies and featured six long-distance terminals. Today there are far fewer long-distance trains, but all are operated from Chicago Union Station, which makes changing trains easier.

Above: Chicago has long been America's railroad capital and dozens of railroads meet here. Above, in 1961, Santa Fe's *Grand Canyon* departs Chicago for the West. Traditionally passenger services were operated by a couple dozen different private companies. After 1971, Amtrak assumed operation of most long-distance services and Chicago developed as its midwestern hub. Today, suburban services are operated by Metra, while the tracks and freight trains are still run by private companies, such as Santa Fe successor, Burlington Northern Santa Fe.

Opposite: Most of Chicago's heavy-rail commuter trains are diesel-powered, though one of the exceptions is the "Metra Electric." This service runs from Randolph Street Station, connecting many communities on Chicago's Southside. Metra Electric uses double-deck electric multiple units (self-propelled cars). In the 1920s, Illinois Central was compelled by the city of Chicago to electrify the service to reduce pollution from steam locomotives. The original electric multiple-units were replaced in the mid-1970s.

Left: Amtrak debuted its fastest train, the *Acela Express*, in December 2000. Twenty specially designed tilting electric trains are used to provide *Acela Express* services between Boston, New York, Philadelphia, and Washington D.C. East of New Haven, Connecticut, the trains are regularly operated at speeds up to 150 mph.

Pages 84-85: Now matter how fast and aerodynamic trains become, one of the most memorable of all time is the old-fashioned circus train. Circus trains carry whole circuses, including animals, performers, tents, and all from city to city. This historic circus train is based at Baraboo, Wisconsin. Today more modern trains are still used by the Ringling Brothers, Barnum and Bailey Circus.

Index

By the same author from
Random House Value Publishing

AMERICA'S RAILROAD STATIONS